P9-CRK-017

OUT OF THIS WORLD
Meet astronaut Peggy Whitson
and find out what it's like to
wear a 300-pound space suit
in zero gravity!

TIME FOR KIDS

ALL ACCESS

YOUR BEHIND-THE-SCENES LOOK AT THE COOLEST PEOPLE, PLACES, AND THINGS!

Project Editors Andrea Woo, Sachin Shenolikar

Creative Director Beth Bugler

Writer Vickie An

Photo Editors Nataki Hewling, Don Heiny

Copy Editor Barbara Collier

Premedia Keith Aurelio (Manager), Charlotte Coco, Kevin Hart

TIME FOR KIDS

Managing Editor Nellie Gonzalez Cutler

Contributing Writers Suzanne Zimbler (White House); David Bjerklie (Antarctica)

TIME HOME ENTERTAINMENT

Publisher Jim Childs
Vice President, Brand & Digital Strategy Steven Sandonato
Executive Director, Marketing Services Carol Pittard
Executive Director, Retail & Special Sales Tom Mifsud
Executive Publishing Director Joy Bomba
Director, Bookazine Development & Marketing Laura Adam
Vice President, Finance Vandana Patel
Publishing Director Megan Pearlman
Assistant General Counsel Simone Procas
Assistant Director, Special Sales Ilene Schreider
Brand Manager Jonathan White
Associate Prepress Manager Alex Voznesenskiy
Associate Production Manager Kimberly Marshall
Associate Project Manager Stephanie Braga

Editorial Director Stephen Koepp
Senior Editor Roe D'Angelo
Copy Chief Rina Bander
Design Manager Anne-Michelle Gallero
Editorial Operations Gina Scauzillo

SPECIAL THANKS: Katherine Barnet, Brad Beatson, Jeremy Biloon, Susan Chodakiewicz, Rose Cirrincione, Assu Etsubneh, Mariana Evans, Christine Font, Susan Hettleman, Hillary Hirsch, David Kahn, Amy Mangus, Nina Mistry, Dave Rozzelle, Ricardo Santiago, Adriana Tierno

Copyright © 2014 Time Home Entertainment Inc.
All TIME FOR KIDS material © 2014 by Time Inc.
TIME FOR KIDS and the red border design are registered trademarks of Time Inc.

For information on TIME FOR KIDS magazine for the
classroom or home, go to TIMEFORKIDS.COM
or call 1-800-777-8600
For subscriptions to SI KIDS, go to
SIKIDS.COM or call 1-800-889-6007

Published by TIME FOR KIDS Books,
An imprint of Time Home Entertainment Inc.
1271 Ave of the Americas, 6th Floor
New York, New York 10020

All rights reserved. No part of this book may be reproduced in any form or by any electronic or mechanical means, including information storage and retrieval systems, without permission in writing from the publisher, except by a reviewer, who may quote brief passages in a review.

ISBN 10: 1-61893-105-9
ISBN 13: 978-1-61893-105-4
Library of Congress Control Number: 2014934078

We welcome your comments and suggestions about TIME FOR KIDS Books. Please write to us at:
TIME FOR KIDS Books, Attention: Book Editors, P.O. Box 11016, Des Moines, IA 50336-1016.
If you would like to order any of our hardcover Collector's Edition books, please call us at
1-800-327-6388 (Monday through Friday, 7 a.m.–8 p.m., or Saturday, 7 a.m.–6 p.m., Central Time).

1 TLF 14

PEOPLE

PLACES

THINGS

Get an up-close look at the folks who have some of the coolest jobs in the world — and beyond!

Peggy Whitson remembers being glued to the TV as astronauts Neil Armstrong and Buzz Aldrin became the first people to step foot on the moon, in July 1969. She was just 9 years old at the time, but a spark had gone off. She wanted to be an astronaut.

Today, Whitson is living her dream. In 2002 and 2007, she blasted off on two six-month missions aboard the International Space Station (ISS). She's performed six space walks and has logged 377 days in space, the most time in orbit for a woman.

Peggy Whitson
ASTRONAUT

She also holds the honor of being the first female commander of the ISS—not to mention her appointment as chief of the Astronaut Corps in 2009, another first for a woman.

And she's not done yet. Whitson says she'd love to go on a third mission to the ISS and perform more space walks. Some heavy-duty training goes into a space walk, especially learning to operate the nearly 300-pound space suit. Astronauts wear the suits to protect against extreme conditions. In space, there is no oxygen. Temperatures fall as low as −250°F and rise as high as 275°F. Small bits of dust and rock fly by at high speeds.

While the suit weighs nothing in space, it still takes skill and physical strength to move and work in it. Here's a closer look at Whitson's suit.

PEOPLE

HARD UPPER TORSO
This section is made out of fiberglass, a hard material. The other parts of the suit attach to it. It also holds a mini-tool carrier. The tools hook on to the suit so that they don't float away during a space walk.

HELMET AND VISOR
The helmet is made of clear, strong plastic. Oxygen flows inside of it so that the astronaut can breathe. The visor fits over the helmet. It has blinders to block the sun, as well as four lamps and a camera.

GLOVES
Rubber fingers on the gloves help an astronaut keep a firm grip on the tools. Fingertip heaters keep the digits toasty. Fabric gloves are worn underneath.

DISPLAYS AND CONTROL MODULE
Astronauts control the oxygen, temperature, and other life-support systems from here. The labels are written in reverse. The suit operator uses a mirror to read them.

WHITE FABRIC
One reason the suit is white is to reflect heat. Another reason is that white is more visible against the blackness of space, so spacewalkers can be spotted easily.

LOWER TORSO
The suit pants come in varying sizes to fit different astronauts. A ring at the waist allows the astronaut to turn his or her body more freely. The red stripes help crew members identify the spacewalkers.

PRIMARY LIFE-SUPPORT SYSTEM
This backpack holds a life-support system that stores oxygen and removes carbon dioxide from the suit. It also contains cooling water, a ventilating fan, a warning system, a radio, and a powerful battery.

SECONDARY OXYGEN PACK
This backup pack is attached to the base of the life-support backpack. It contains two emergency tanks with enough oxygen for 30 minutes.

ELECTRICAL HARNESS
Worn inside the suit, the harness connects to the radio and medical monitors found in the life-support backpack. It keeps track of an astronaut's breathing rate, heart rate, and temperature during a space walk.

ARMS
The arms come in different sizes. The sleeve is where the mirror used to read the displays and control module can be found. A checklist on the wrist has the tasks for the space walk.

IN-SUIT DRINK BAG
Velcro is used to attach a pouch filled with drinking water inside the upper torso. A straw comes up into the helmet for easy sipping.

LAYERS OF PROTECTION
The suit has 14 layers to guard against overheating, radiation, and small debris. The layers also help regulate air pressure inside the suit.

LIQUID-COOLING AND VENTILATION GARMENT

Astronauts wear this stretchy pair of spandex long johns under their spacesuits. It's not to keep them warm—it's to keep them cool! The garment is laced with thin plastic tubes, 300 of them to be precise.

COOLING TUBES

Chilled water is pumped into the tubes near the astronaut's skin. The tubes run around the crew member's whole body. This helps remove excess body heat during a space walk.

VENTILATION DUCTS

Vents in the cooling garment draw sweat away from the astronaut's body. But it doesn't go too far. The sweat gets recycled into the water-cooling system.

COMMUNICATIONS CARRIER ASSEMBLY

This fabric "Snoopy cap" contains small microphones and speakers that allow the astronaut to talk and listen to others without using his or her hands. It is worn underneath the helmet and visor.

MAXIMUM ABSORPTION GARMENT

There's no time for restroom breaks during a space walk. Astronauts wear an adult-size diaper underneath their suit in case of bathroom emergencies.

LONG UNDERWEAR

Crew members wear an additional pair of long underwear beneath the liquid-cooling garment for comfort.

Life in Space

There's a reason astronauts train for months before traveling to the International Space Station (ISS). Space is a tough place to live in! Take it from those who have spent time aboard the floating science laboratory, including NASA's Peggy Whitson. "You train for the bits and pieces," she explains, "but until you get there, it's hard to predict what it's going to feel like."

The station circles between 200 to 250 miles above Earth at a speed of 17,500 miles per hour. There is very little gravity in space. So it's not surprising that the body can take a while to adjust. "It's always interesting to see the new guys arrive on the space station," Whitson recalls. "They're like gangly teenagers." Oftentimes, astronauts can feel dizzy, nauseated, or tired when they first arrive in space. But once they do adapt, "it becomes home, and floating becomes second nature," says Whitson, adding, "It's an amazing structure that we live in up there."

The impressive orbiting outpost is the largest man-made object in space. It weighs nearly a million pounds and spans the area of an entire football field. The first crew arrived on the ISS in 2000. A rotating crew of astronauts and cosmonauts from the United States, Russia, Canada, Japan, and Europe has been living on the craft ever since. Here's a look inside life on the space station.

BUILDING A HOME

Astronauts haven't just lived and worked on the ISS. They also assembled it. Construction began in 1998 with the launch of the first component, the Zarya control module, on a Russian rocket. (*Zarya* means "sunrise" in Russian.) Several nations have contributed to the building of the outpost over the years. On March 1, 2011, the crew used a robotic arm to connect the final U.S. piece, a storage closet. Here, NASA astronauts Alvin Drew and Steve Bowen prep for the installation and perform other tasks during a space walk, on February 28, 2011.

SCIENCE GUYS

When they're not taking walks in space, the crew conducts research—lots of it. Many of the studies focus on how the human body reacts to living in microgravity for long periods. Understanding this is key if people are to travel farther into space, to places such as Mars. Japanese astronaut Koichi Wakata measures his oxygen intake while he exercises during one such experiment in the Destiny lab, on November 26, 2013.

STAYING IN SHAPE

NASA astronaut Sunita Williams wears a harness as she goes for a run on the Combined Operational Load Bearing External Resistance Treadmill (COLBERT) in the Tranquility node, on August 4, 2012. Muscles and bones can become weaker in reduced gravity. To keep themselves healthy and fit while in space, crew members spend an average of two hours exercising every day.

GOBBLE, GOBBLE

NASA astronauts Michael Hopkins (far left) and Rick Mastracchio dig into a Thanksgiving day feast of turkey with all the trimmings, in the Unity node, on November 28, 2013. Many of the meals come freeze-dried or dehydrated. This gives the food a longer shelf life. To rehydrate the items, hot water must be added before heating the packets in a special oven. Other dishes come ready-to-eat in foil pouches that just need to be warmed.

BREAK TIME!

It's not all work and no play. Astronauts find time to have fun on the ISS too. Canadian astronaut Chris Hadfield enjoys strumming his guitar during downtimes. Hadfield made headlines in May 2013 when he posted on YouTube a music video of himself singing a version of David Bowie's "Space Oddity." The video quickly went viral and had received more than 21 million views as of March 2014.

WINDOWS ON THE WORLD

The Cupola control tower of the ISS offers a stunning panoramic look at Earth. From here, astronauts can observe space-walking activities, communicate with crew members, and control the robotic arm. But sometimes, it's nice to just sit back and take in the view, as NASA astronaut Karen Nyberg does here on November 4, 2013.

SLEEP TIGHT

To keep from floating away as they snooze, crew members tuck themselves into sleeping bags inside cozy individual compartments. Here, European Space Agency astronaut Paolo Nespoli (near right) and NASA astronauts Scott Kelly and Catherine (Cady) Coleman peek out of their sleeping quarters in the Harmony node to check out the decorations on Christmas Day 2010.

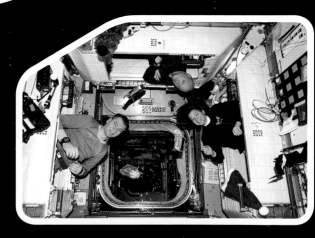

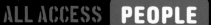

Joe Cicero
FIREFIGHTER

Everyday Heroes

All crew members wear a **PASS DEVICE**. *PASS* stands for personal alert safety system. If a firefighter stops moving for a specified period of time, a loud alarm sounds. This alerts others that the person needs help.

The beam from an **LED FLASHLIGHT** cuts through smoke, giving firefighters better vision when searching for civilians.

This tool, called a **HOOK**, is used to pull materials down from ceilings and walls. This one is six feet long. A 20-foot hook is also kept on the rig for high ceilings.

F or Joe Cicero, fighting fires is a family affair. His father, grandfather, and uncles all were firemen for the Fire Department of the City of New York (FDNY). So as a kid, he dreamed of being one too. "Growing up, I always went to the firehouse when my father was working," Cicero recalls. "Firefighting's in the bloodline. I was drawn to it."

Today, Cicero proudly carries on his family's legacy. He's a firefighter for Engine 155/Ladder 78, in Staten Island. In this line of work, you never know what dangers each day may bring. At any given moment, the company can be called to any kind of emergency, from fires and car accidents to building collapses. That's why preparation is key. At the station, firefighters constantly review situations and run drills. "The training never ends," Cicero says.

Having the right equipment is equally important for the job, he says. Firefighters wear special gear to keep them safe as they battle a blaze. Cicero gave All Access a special look at his uniform and tools.

Firefighters wear a **HELMET** made of hard plastic for protection from falling objects. A visor and ear flaps shield the eyes and ears.

While a **BUNKER COAT** isn't fireproof, it is designed to withstand heat and fire for short periods. The protective layer gives firefighters enough time to get into a burning building to fight the flames and look for survivors, and then to get out safely.

These thick, leather **GLOVES** guard hands from cuts and burns.

A **FACE MASK** keeps fire, steam, and hot embers away from the face. The **HOOD** is worn under the helmet to protect the head, neck, and ears.

A hose connects the mask to an **AIR-SUPPLY TANK** worn on the back, and a regulator controls the flow of fresh air.

Firefighters wear sturdy **BOOTS** made of leather or rubber to protect their feet from heavy falling objects. Steel toes add extra protection.

In the House

To firefighters, a fire station represents much more than just a workplace. They spend so much time there that it becomes "a home away from home," says Jeff Franzreb, who along with Cicero is a member of the FDNY's Engine 155/Ladder 78. The fire station is where firefighters rest, where they eat their meals, and where they relax when they're not out on emergencies or running drills. Because of this, everyone takes great care in keeping every inch of the station neat and tidy, especially the apparatus floor. That's where the trucks are parked and the gear is stored. Read on for a closer look inside the fire station.

THE COMPANY
This Staten Island fire station houses two companies: Engine 155 and Ladder 78. What's the difference? It's all in the rigs. Fire engines transport the hoses and nozzles needed to pump water onto a fire. Meanwhile, ladder trucks carry multiple ladders and tools that firefighters need to enter a burning structure and pull people out.

FIRST RESPONDERS
In addition to carrying the hoses, the fire engine is also equipped with emergency medical supplies. Firefighters are certified first responders who are trained to provide emergency care. Often an engine will get to an accident scene faster than an ambulance. In that case, firefighters would begin administering aid, and the paramedics would take over when they arrived.

MORE THAN 3,000 FEET OF HOSE!

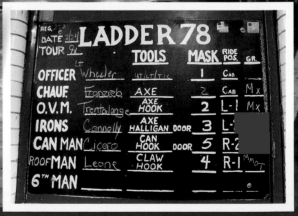

THE DAY'S DUTIES
The riding list shows each firefighter's assigned task on the rig. The ladder has six main positions. The officer oversees the response and leads the team into the fire. The chauffeur drives the rig and operates the ladder. The outside vent person creates an opening for smoke and heat to escape. The irons and can positions gain access into a building to locate trapped civilians. And the roof position reports on conditions from up top.

THE LADDER CAN EXTEND TO 100 FEET!

THE FIRE POLE!

BOOTS AND PANTS, READY TO GO!

ALWAYS PREPARED

Once the alarm bell sounds, it's time to go, go, go! Firefighters make sure they're never caught off guard. One timesaving trick: They leave their bunker pants scrunched down on the ground over their boots. Then all they need to do is step in and pull up, and they're dressed! Some stations also have fire poles. The poles connect the top floors of a fire station to the apparatus floor for a speedy descent.

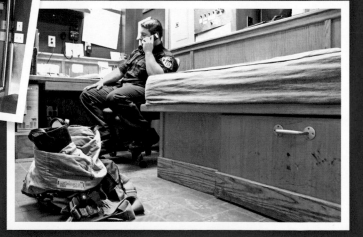

KITCHEN CAMARADERIE

When on duty, the fire station crew cooks and eats meals together in the kitchen. "It's the hub of the firehouse," Franzreb explains. "It's where you have all your laughs." The camaraderie formed by the group is useful out in the field, too. "It helps when you go into these situations with a 'brother,'" says Franzreb. The housewatch (far right) is where all the emergency calls are received. When an alarm comes in, the person on housewatch duty rings the fire station bell. This alerts everyone that it's time to put their gear on and head out!

The Magic of Makeup

Peter Swords King

HAIR AND MAKEUP DESIGNER

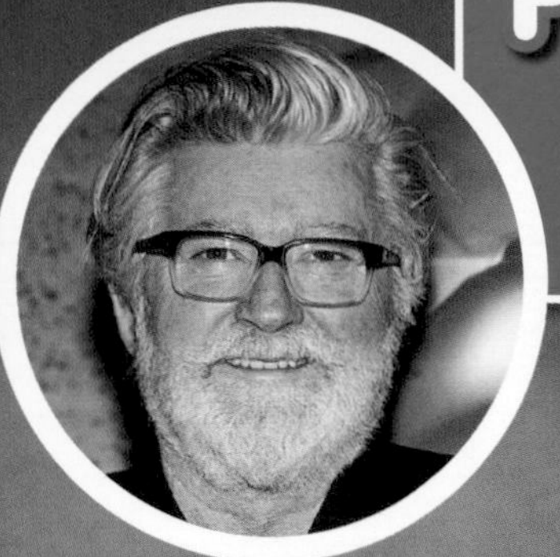

Nori
Fili
Dori
Bofur
Gloin
Dwalin

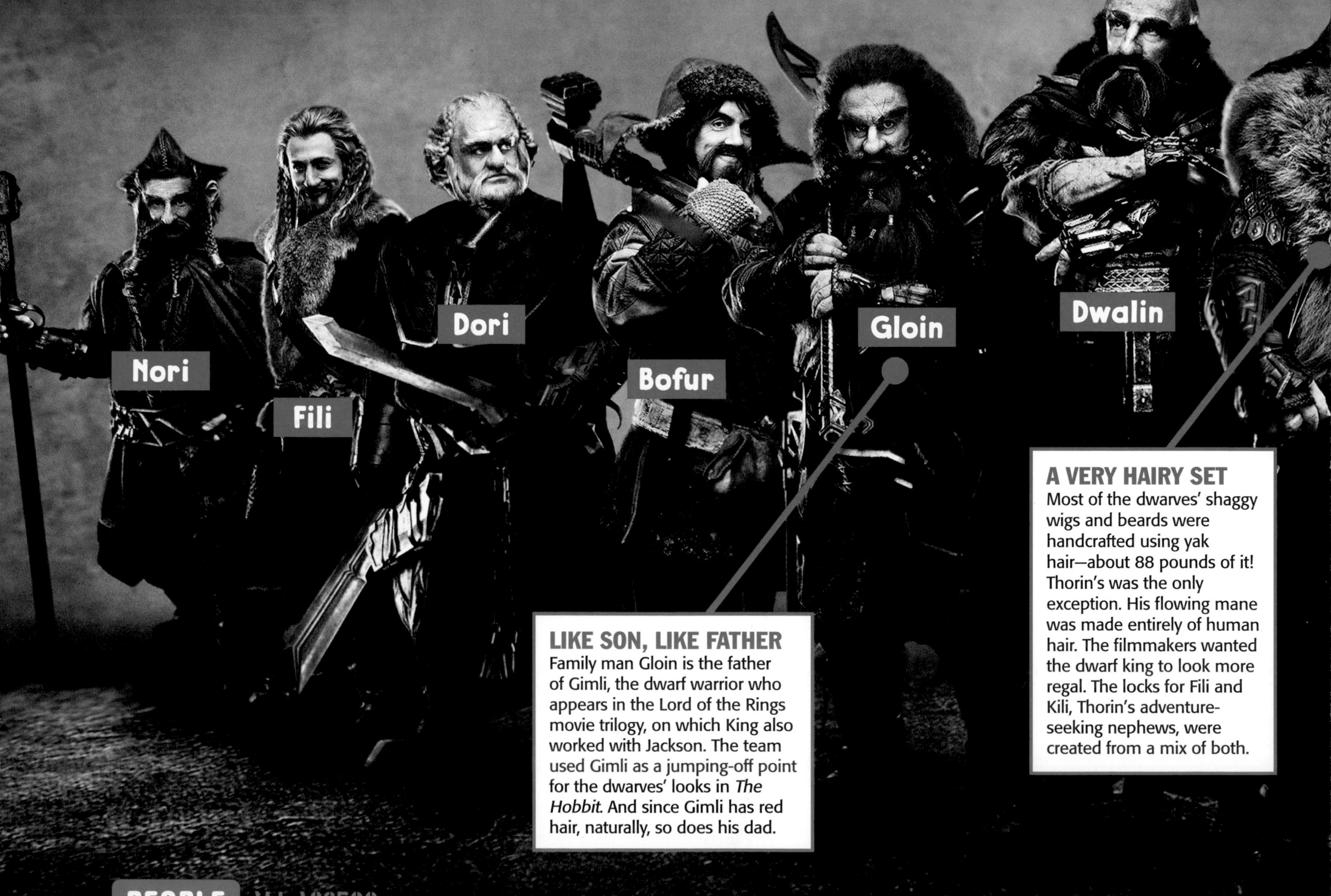

LIKE SON, LIKE FATHER
Family man Gloin is the father of Gimli, the dwarf warrior who appears in the Lord of the Rings movie trilogy, on which King also worked with Jackson. The team used Gimli as a jumping-off point for the dwarves' looks in *The Hobbit.* And since Gimli has red hair, naturally, so does his dad.

A VERY HAIRY SET
Most of the dwarves' shaggy wigs and beards were handcrafted using yak hair—about 88 pounds of it! Thorin's was the only exception. His flowing mane was made entirely of human hair. The filmmakers wanted the dwarf king to look more regal. The locks for Fili and Kili, Thorin's adventure-seeking nephews, were created from a mix of both.

Thorin

Balin

Oin

Bombur

Bifur

Ori

Kili

BEHIND THE BEARD

The team considered giving Balin a mustache before ultimately deciding against it. Not to worry, though. He still sports an ample amount of facial hair. The wise dwarf's snowy beard, while simpler than some of the others, suits his gentle nature.

MAKING FACES

It took about 8,800 pounds of silicone rubber to produce the facial prosthetics for the films. The rotund Bombur, whose favorite pastimes include cooking and eating, is the only dwarf who requires full-face prosthetics. The others needed only "T-pieces," which covered the actors' foreheads and noses.

MAMA'S BOY

The older dwarves boasted fuller, more sophisticated facial hair than their younger comrades. In fact, sweet-natured Ori still wears the purple ribbons his mother tied into his hair before he set out on his journey. Although having a small, scruffy beard may have been a blessing in disguise— for the actor, at least. Many of the dwarves' beards weighed so much that they had to be strapped to the actors' heads.

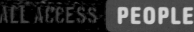

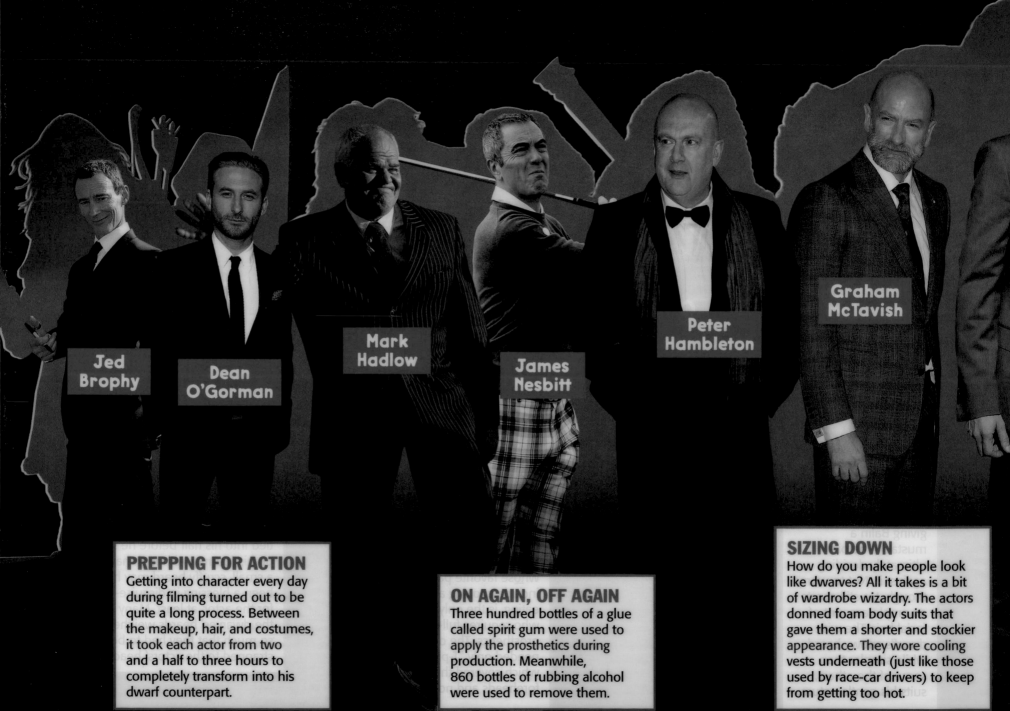

Jed Brophy

Dean O'Gorman

Mark Hadlow

James Nesbitt

Peter Hambleton

Graham McTavish

PREPPING FOR ACTION
Getting into character every day during filming turned out to be quite a long process. Between the makeup, hair, and costumes, it took each actor from two and a half to three hours to completely transform into his dwarf counterpart.

ON AGAIN, OFF AGAIN
Three hundred bottles of a glue called spirit gum were used to apply the prosthetics during production. Meanwhile, 860 bottles of rubbing alcohol were used to remove them.

SIZING DOWN
How do you make people look like dwarves? All it takes is a bit of wardrobe wizardry. The actors donned foam body suits that gave them a shorter and stockier appearance. They wore cooling vests underneath (just like those used by race-car drivers) to keep from getting too hot.

Move aside, Gandalf! There's a new wizard in town, and his name is Peter Swords King. But instead of casting spells, he performs wondrous feats of movie magic with his makeup brushes. King is the Oscar-winning hair and makeup designer for the Hobbit movie trilogy, based on the stories by J.R.R. Tolkien. The first installments, *An Unexpected Journey* and *The Desolation of Smaug*, follow hobbit Bilbo Baggins, wizard Gandalf, and a company of dwarves on a quest to reclaim the dwarf kingdom Erebor from a wicked dragon. To step into their roles, all of the films' stars had to undergo big transformations. The 13 actors who played the dwarves received the most dramatic makeovers of all. King's team worked closely with director Peter Jackson and special-effects company Weta Workshop to design distinct looks that matched the personality of each dwarf.

Then came the real work: physically bringing the characters to life. This included creating all the necessary prosthetic makeup, beards, and wigs. "For each dwarf, we made seven wigs—that is 91 wigs total!" King says. And that's just one aspect of turning someone into a Middle-earth dwarf. Keep reading to learn more about the process and to see what the actors really look like—it's surprising!

Richard Armitage

Ken Stott

John Callen

Stephen Hunter

William Kircher

Adam Brown

Aidan Turner

BULKING UP
Dwarves have bigger noggins than the average human's. So the actors wore foam cowls under their already bulky wigs to give the illusion of a larger skull. The ears were positioned further out from the head to add extra width. They also wore prosthetic arms and hands.

DETAILS, DETAILS
To perfect the looks, King held several "show-and-tell" sessions with Jackson and the department heads well before filming even began. In these meetings, the actors would dress in full makeup and costume, and the team would note any alterations needed. These changes could range anywhere from making the beards longer to adding more "blood vessels" to the prosthetics.

Her Wild Life

Dr. Suzan Murray
CHIEF VETERINARIAN, NATIONAL ZOO

It can be tough taking care of one pet. Can you imagine what it's like to be in charge of 2,000 of them? It's all in a day's work for Suzan Murray. She's the chief veterinarian at the Smithsonian National Zoo, in Washington, D.C. Since 2001, Murray has headed the team of vets that oversees the health care of the zoo's entire wildlife collection. That includes the zoo's biggest star, the giant panda.

In addition to her main duties, Murray leads training, research, and conservation programs. After working with so many species, does she have a favorite? No, she says. She likes them all! "I love elephants, Japanese giant salamanders, flamingos, primates, the big cats," Murray lists. "Really, any animal we're working with holds fascination for me." Here's how Murray's team cares for the animals at the zoo.

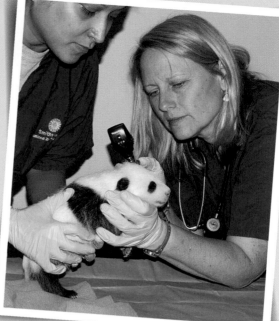

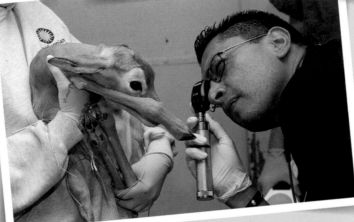

CHECKUP TIME!

"Vet exams, especially on small animals, are very similar to what you would do for a human," Murray (above, right) explains. "We go through all the systems—the eyes, ears, nose, and throat. We listen to the heart, examine the abdomen, and check for a range of motions. We check the animal's temperature as well."

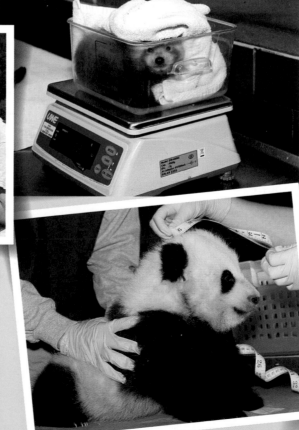

SIZING THEM UP

There's a lot of documentation about how quickly children should grow. But when it comes to endangered species like giant pandas, there's not as much information. That's why it's important for zoo vets to collect and share as much data as possible. "We record everything: an animal's weight and length, when its eyes open, when its teeth come in, when it learns how to do physical activities," says Murray. The panda keepers even train the cubs to help. The bears step onto the scales to weigh themselves!

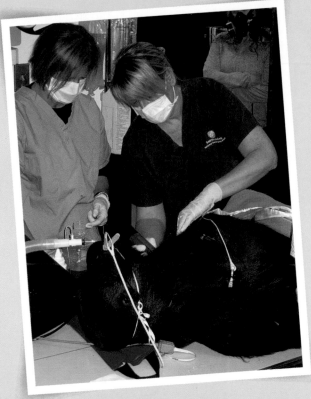

CHOW DOWN!

Each species has its own dietary requirements, so the zoo employs nutrition specialists to create and manage specific diet plans for all the animals. The nutritionists prepare the foods and make sure the animals get all the necessary vitamins, minerals, and other nutrients. They work very closely with the veterinarians, the keepers, and the curators to keep the animals healthy.

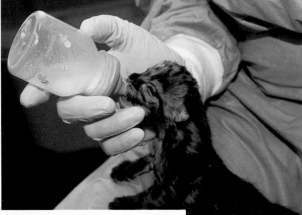

CALLING IN SICK

Animals have sick days too. But Murray (above, right) says surgery is rare. "Usually, the only time we have to do a surgical procedure is if an animal is injured, or if we have to investigate something like a mass in the liver or an intestinal blockage. That's the only time we would need to open up an animal."

My, How They Grow!

The National Zoo's giant panda Mei Xiang (may shong) gave birth to panda cub Bao Bao on August 23, 2013. The little fuzz ball is getting bigger every day! This chart shows how panda cubs grow.

Newborn

Pandas weigh from three to five ounces and measure seven inches long when they are born—about the size of a stick of butter.

Two Weeks

After the first week, the cub starts to develop the familiar black marks on its skin. Then by week two, its fur begins to grow.

Three Weeks

At three weeks, the cub looks like a miniature version of its parents. It may begin to crawl. At one month, its eyes start to open.

Three Months

Now the cub can stand and walk a bit. Its eyesight and hearing improve, and its teeth come in. By month four, the cub can run and play.

Baby Boom

The National Zoo and the Smithsonian Conservation Biology Institute welcome lots of new animals every year. Among the many cuddly newborns in recent years: clouded leopards, red pandas, and of course, giant panda cub Bao Bao. She was the first panda to survive birth at the zoo since 2005. "It's exciting when there's a newborn panda at the zoo," says Murray. "It really shows off all that we do here. And the cubs are so charismatic and adorable." Judging by the thousands of people who watch the zoo's panda cam each day, the world agrees.

GIANT PANDA

CLOUDED LEOPARDS

CUBAN CROCODILE

DAMA GAZELLE

RED PANDAS

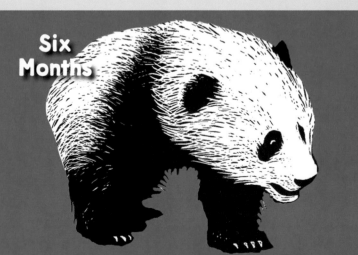

Six Months

At five months, the cub will start following its mom around the den and mimicking her as she eats bamboo. At this age, the cub can also be found climbing trees. By six months, the cub will begin eating solid foods.

One Year

By the time the cub reaches its first birthday, it will weigh from 50 to 60 pounds. In the wild, cubs leave their mothers between the 18-month and two-year marks. Adult pandas can weigh as much as 250 pounds.

PLACES

Join us on a tour of some really cool places that most kids don't get to see!

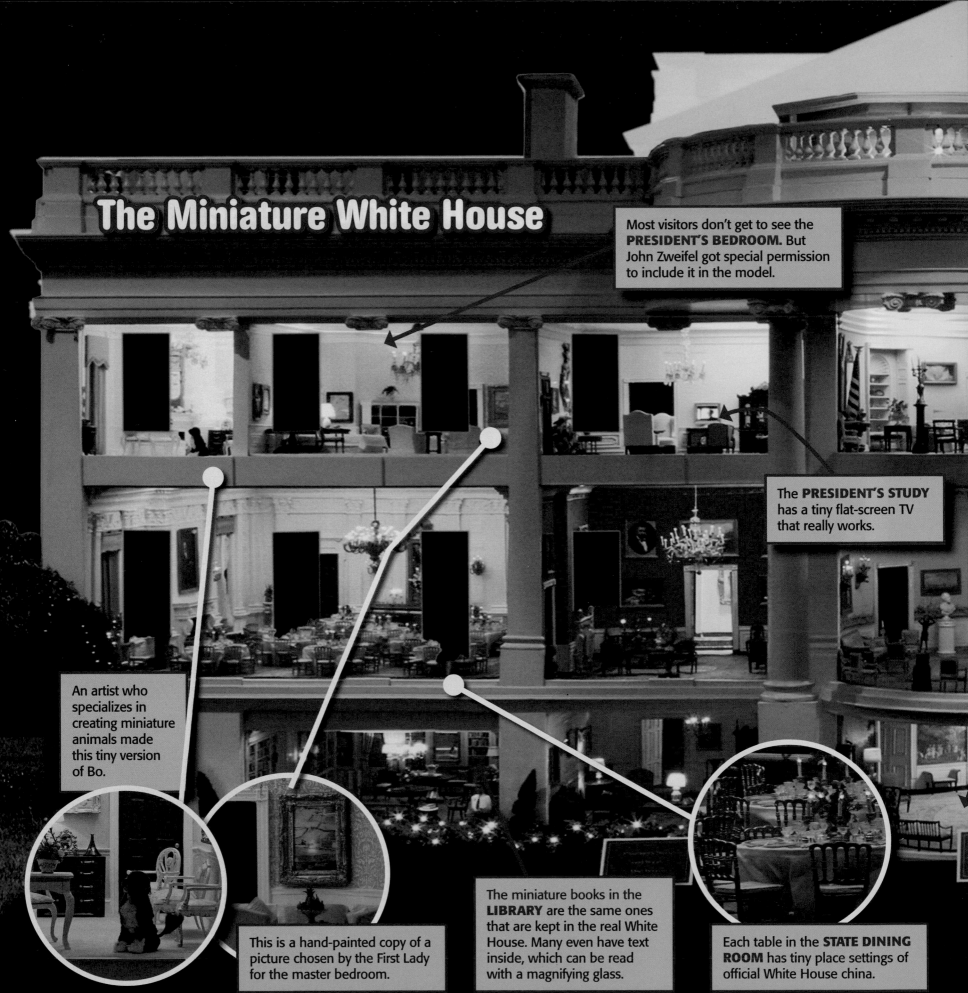

The Miniature White House

Most visitors don't get to see the **PRESIDENT'S BEDROOM**. But John Zweifel got special permission to include it in the model.

The **PRESIDENT'S STUDY** has a tiny flat-screen TV that really works.

An artist who specializes in creating miniature animals made this tiny version of Bo.

This is a hand-painted copy of a picture chosen by the First Lady for the master bedroom.

The miniature books in the **LIBRARY** are the same ones that are kept in the real White House. Many even have text inside, which can be read with a magnifying glass.

Each table in the **STATE DINING ROOM** has tiny place settings of official White House china.

The **BLUE ROOM** is the customary place for presidents to formally greet guests. Like the actual room, this mini-version is decorated with a fragrant floral arrangement.

Zweifel has included such details as the roller-skate marks left on the floor of the **EAST ROOM** by President Jimmy Carter's daughter Amy in 1976. Years later, when the White House floor was fixed, Zweifel polished this floor too.

Tens of thousands of volunteers have spent more than 600,000 hours working on the model over the years. A 2½-inch carved table in the **LINCOLN BEDROOM** took Zweifel's son Jack 160 hours to complete.

The rugs are, stitch for stitch, exact copies of the originals. Some, like this one in the **DIPLOMATIC RECEPTION ROOM,** took years to create. The rug contains symbols of the 50 states.

Would you like to tour the White House? John Zweifel has dedicated his life to making that possible. He has spent 50 years creating a miniature replica of the famous house. Except for the location of the library—which is actually behind the last room on the bottom right—his model is exactly like the real White House. Even the photos in the Oval Office are the same as the ones President Barack Obama displays! Zweifel has visited the president's home hundreds of times. His version is in perfect proportion to the real White House. One inch on the model equals one foot of the real thing. "I just want to have everybody who ever wanted to see that house see it," Zweifel says.

The model is currrently at the Presidents Hall of Fame, in Clermont, Florida.

Google HQ

Google's World

Google is known for being one of the best places to work. Take a look around, and it's easy to see why! The campuses look more like playgrounds than typical offices. There's a reason for that. Studies show that when employees have more freedom during work hours, productivity goes up. The Internet giant has taken note. "Every office is designed with the same purpose in mind," says Google's David Radcliffe, "to create amazing work environments that help Googlers perform at their best every day."

Radcliffe is in charge of setting up new Google headquarters. The tech company has more than 70 locations worldwide, and no two offices are exactly alike. However, they all share these "Googley" elements: whimsical meeting areas, plenty of break rooms, free meals (plus unlimited snacks!), and more. These are some of our favorite Google offices across the globe, starting with the Googleplex (above), in Mountain View, California, where it all began.

Work! 🔍

Each Google office tries to mirror its home city. For example, at Google New York (left), one communal work area is set up as a tiny New York City apartment. Look closely, and you'll even see framed photos, cookware, and a pet cat. Meanwhile, across the Atlantic, in France, designers for the Paris headquarters (below) paid homage to the classic French Citroën 2CV car by converting one into a workspace.

Meet!

Conference rooms come in all shapes and sizes at Google's offices. These open, casual spaces are designed to bring coworkers together and help inspire creativity. At the headquarters in Zürich, Switzerland, Googlers convene in colorful ski gondolas and tunnel-themed workstations (right). If privacy is needed, Google's got that covered too. Hidden behind the shelves in the New York office's library (above): secret meeting spots. *Shhh!*

Googlers don't just work at the various headquarters—they also run the company's data centers. These facilities house the servers that keep Google.com online. Here, an employee at the data center in The Dalles, Oregon (left), repairs an overheated computer.

Move!

Traveling from one end of campus to the other can gobble up precious time. Google's solution? Bicycles—lots of them! At the headquarters in Amsterdam, the Netherlands (right), Googlers ride their bikes indoors as well. As for moving between floors, slides, like this one in Zürich (below), make for quicker access—and loads of fun.

Speaking of fun—it's encouraged! Employee health and well-being are important to the company, says Radcliffe. So Google offers several ways for staffers to stay active. Billiards, foosball, and table tennis can be found in most offices. Some campuses also feature bowling alleys, beach-volleyball courts, and yoga classes. Miniature golf courses, like this one at Google Toronto, in Canada, are popular too.

Recharge!

Need a reboot? No problem. Googleplex staff can just head to the EnergyPods. These special nap stations give those in need of recharging a cozy place to catch a few winks. When it's time to wake up, the high-tech pod uses light and gentle vibrations to rouse snoozing Googlers.

Amazing Amazon

No place on Earth teems with more life than the Amazon rain forest. Several million plant and animal species call this mighty jungle home, and scientists are discovering more all the time. In fact, more than 400 new species, including a purring monkey and a vegetarian piranha, were found from 2010 to 2013 alone. These finds aren't too surprising, though. After all, there's a lot of ground to uncover in the Amazon. The massive forest extends into eight countries in South America: Brazil, Bolivia, Colombia, Ecuador, Guyana, Peru, Suriname, and Venezuela, as well as French Guiana, an overseas territory of France. It's an area totaling 2.3 million square miles. That's twice the size of India!

But despite its vast scope, the Amazon faces many threats. Climate change and deforestation are causing the rain forest to shrink at alarming rates. About 20% of the original forest is already gone. That's bad news for the critters that rely on the tropical environment to survive. As their habitats vanish, a growing number of animals are becoming endangered and even extinct every year. That's why it's more important than ever to preserve what's left of these majestic jungles.

One in 10 of all the world's known species inhabits the Amazon. Each of the four layers of the rain forest—the emergent layer, the canopy, the understory, and the forest floor—is alive with its own unique ecosystem of vegetation and wildlife. Here's a behind-the-trees peek at some of the Amazon's most fascinating creatures.

Amazon Rain Forest
SOUTH AMERICA

TOUCAN

The toucan lives in the canopy but can sometimes be found foraging for food in the emergent layer. It uses the tip of its large, colorful beak to pluck the ripest fruits. Then with a quick tilt of its head, it gobbles the fruit down.

EMERGENT LAYER

The emergent layer is the highest part of the rain forest. The trees that make up this layer can grow as much as 200 feet tall. With sturdy roots and trunks measuring up to 16 feet around, these towering giants can weather everything Mother Nature throws at them, from high temperatures and pouring rain to howling winds. Several species of birds, bats, and monkeys make their homes high up in the emergent layer, where they find a safe haven from predators.

KINKAJOU

These big-eyed mammals may hang from trees like monkeys, but they're actually related to raccoons. Kinkajous are also called honey bears. Can you guess why? Because they use their long tongues to slurp honey and nectar from beehives and flowers.

CANOPY

Located 60 feet to 150 feet aboveground is the canopy. Many of the Amazon's critters—monkeys, birds, snakes, tree frogs, insects, and more—live their entire lives in this part of the rain forest, where food is abundant. The canopy's dense network of leaves, vines, and branches works as a roof, filtering out up to 80% of the incoming sunlight.

CAQUETÁ TITÍ MONKEY

Scientists discovered this species of tití monkey, which is critically endangered, only in the past 10 years. The babies have a paw-sitively charming trait: They purr like kittens when they're happy.

BLUE MORPHO BUTTERFLY

Despite its name, this dazzling butterfly isn't truly blue. Its wings are covered in tiny scales that reflect blue light. This gives the insect its shimmery azure appearance.

UNDERSTORY

Since the canopy blocks out so much light, plants in the understory have adapted to the darkness by growing large, flat leaves to capture the sun's rays. Trees, shrubs, and other plants in this part of the rain forest don't grow taller than 12 feet. The understory is home to the largest and most diverse concentration of insects, which, along with other animals, help disperse seeds and pollinate flowers.

STICK INSECT

Talk about masters of disguise! Stick insects' bodies mimic the twigs on which they live. If needed, the bugs can also shed a limb or two to escape predators.

TAPIR

The tapir's upper lip and nose combine to form a small, prehensile snout. The animal uses its trunk to pluck tasty fruits and leaves from branches.

FOREST FLOOR

The absence of sunshine on the forest floor means it's always dark and damp. There are some creatures that don't mind living in the shadows, though. Some of the Amazon's biggest and smallest animals spend their days foraging on the forest floor. But aside from mosses, very few plants grow in this layer. Decomposing leaves and organisms litter the ground, creating nutrients for the soil.

SPIDER MONKEY

Spider monkeys use their strong prehensile, or grasping, tails to help them swing nimbly from tree to tree. It's easy to see how the species got its name. The monkeys look like giant spiders when hanging upside down from the branches!

SCARLET MACAW

These noisy birds are famous for their bold plumage. Believe it or not, the bright feathers help the birds blend perfectly into the rain forest's vibrant backdrop.

HARPY EAGLE

In Greek, *harpy* means "snatcher." It's a fitting name for the majestic eagle species. Armed with a hooked beak, sharp talons, and speed, this fierce predator can easily snatch up an unsuspecting monkey or sloth for dinner.

GOLDEN POISON DART FROG

If you spot one of these guys in the jungle, take a hop back! This species of poison frog is one of the most toxic creatures on Earth. The indigenous Emberá people of Colombia dip their blowgun darts in its venom for hunting. The tiniest drop of this frog's poison can take down a small animal.

THREE-TOED SLOTH

Sloths love catching their z's. These sleepy creatures spend up to 20 hours a day snoozing in the trees. Even when they're awake, sloths stay very still—so much so that algae grows on their fur!

OCELOT

Known for their luxurious spotted coats, ocelots were once hunted to the brink of extinction for their fur. Conservation laws have since allowed the species to bounce back. But habitat loss still poses a threat to the cats and other animals.

EMERALD TREE BOA

Call it a sixth sense. The emerald tree boa has small holes in its snout that serve as heat sensors. This helps the snake detect prey from a distance.

CAPYBARA

How long can you hold your breath? Probably not as long as capybaras! These semiaquatic animals can stay underwater for up to five minutes at a time. The rodents' partially webbed feet also make them expert swimmers.

LEAFCUTTER ANTS

They're little but incredibly strong! These ants can carry leaves that weigh several times their own body weight.

JAGUAR

Unlike other Big Cats, this ferocious feline doesn't like to chase down its dinner. Instead, it prefers to hide and wait for its prey to get close before roaring into action.

Second Avenue Subway
NEW YORK, NEW YORK

Tunnel Vision

New York City streets bustle with activity at all hours of the day. The same can be said for underneath the city too. In 2013, more than 1.7 billion people hitched a ride on the city's subway, making it the nation's busiest transit system. Ridership is rising with every passing year, which also means increasingly packed subway cars. So to help ease overcrowding underground, the city's Metropolitan Transportation Authority (MTA) is adding a new subway line—one that will run on Manhattan's east side from 125th Street to the Financial District downtown.

The city presented its first official proposal to build this new line, known as the Second Avenue subway, back in 1929. However, plans were derailed in the 1930s because of the Great Depression. The project has been revived several times over the years. And each time, outside forces caused city leaders to postpone plans.

After so many delays, some thought the Second Avenue subway would never be built. But today, the city is seeing a light at the end of the tunnel. On April 12, 2007, the MTA finally broke ground on the first phase of construction, which is expected to be completed by 2016. Here's a sneak peek at the progress.

DIGGING IN

The MTA is using a tunnel-boring machine to mine the Second Avenue subway's two tunnels. The machine weighs 485 tons, or 970,000 pounds, and is two and a half city blocks long. Its powerful, 22-foot-diameter rotating cutterhead can burrow through a variety of soils and hard bedrock. In this April 7, 2011, photo, the machine's operators continue mining the second tunnel after excavation is finished on the first.

BREAKTHROUGH

Workers spray water on a rock wall as the tunnel-boring machine breaks through to the existing subway system, on September 22, 2011. The water helps reduce the amount of dust particles in the air. It's a milestone day for the construction crew as tunneling for the project's first phase reaches completion. The MTA launched the tunnel-boring machine on May 14, 2010. The machine mined an average of 60 feet a day, totaling 7,789 feet of tunneling during phase one.

SAFETY FIRST

Construction work, especially underground, can be dangerous. As a safety precaution, the hundreds of crew members employed on the Second Avenue subway project all wear helmets, gloves, reflective vests, and protective glasses.

VIEW FROM ABOVE

Most of the construction on the Second Avenue subway takes place far beneath the city streets. But, of course, riders need a way to enter the subway system from aboveground too. This photo shows a bird's-eye view of the work being done on the 96th Street station entrance, on January 10, 2012.

MOVING THE EARTH

To remove debris from the construction site, workers use a machine called a crawler loader. By the end of phase one, 15 million cubic feet of rock and 6 million cubic feet of soil will have been carved out from beneath the city. In this image from March 20, 2012, workers build the cavern that will house the 72nd Street station. The main cavern, located nine stories beneath New York City, is big enough to fit 55,000 elephants!

DOWN THE HOLE

This elevator cage at the 72nd Street cavern takes people down to the construction site from the street level.

WATERPROOFING

A crew works on a waterproofing project at the 86th Street station, on March 15, 2014. To prevent moisture from seeping into the tunnel foundation, workers must install a special membrane on the walls.

PROGRESS REPORT

This photo from February 22, 2014, shows the progress of the 86th Street cavern. The Second Avenue subway will stretch more than eight miles when all four phases of the project are complete. The MTA says phase one is on track so far to meet its December 2016 deadline.

UNDER THE WIRE

It takes many skilled workers, from laborers and machine operators to surveyors and welders, to build a complete subway system. Here, electrical contractors do wiring work in the tunnels, on May 12, 2012.

The Tale of T. rex

What do you see when you picture a *Tyrannosaurus rex*? Do you see a snarling, massive, 10,000-pound giant? Most people would. Like all animals, though, even this mighty dinosaur king took baby steps at some point.

Scientists know very little about the famous dinosaur's wonder years. Only a handful of young *T. rex* fossils have ever been unearthed. But these unanswered questions only feed the public's fascination, says Luis Chiappe. Chiappe is the director of the Dinosaur Institute at the Natural History Museum of Los Angeles County, in California. He curated the museum's renovated Dinosaur Hall, which features more than 300 dinosaur specimens.

At the heart of the galleries is the Growth Series. The exhibit features a trio of rare juvenile *T. rex* skeletons. "When you put these three *T. rex* fossils together, plus others that have been found, you get a much better understanding of the animal," Chiappe told TFK. So what clues do these prehistoric remains hold about the mysterious life of young *Tyrannosaurus rex*? Flip the page to find out. But first, see what these three dinosaurs may have looked like once upon a time.

North America
65 MILLION YEARS AGO

SUB-ADULT T. REX

T. rex last roamed the river valleys of what is now North America about 65 million years ago, during the late Cretaceous period. *Tyrannosaurus* means "tyrant lizard." It's a fitting name for this fearsome predator. The illustrated dino to the left shows what *T. rex* possibly looked like in its late teens—with still a long way to grow. An adult *T. rex* could stand as tall as 20 feet and measure up to 40 feet long, making it one of the largest meat-eating dinosaurs to walk the Earth. Sure, *T. rex* had tiny arms. But its powerful hind limbs, bone-crushing jaw, and heightened sense of smell made hunting prey a cinch. Scientists believe the dinosaur could gulp down more than 500 pounds of meat in a single bite! The duck-billed edmontosaurus and triceratops were often on the menu. The Growth Series shows the tyrannosaur trio grouped around the carcass of an edmontosaurus, giving a little peek at dinosaur life.

BABY T. REX

Even as a toddler, *T. rex* proved to be pretty intimidating. In life, this not-so-little tyke weighed 66 pounds and measured 11 feet from head to tail. Still, as a hatchling, *T. rex* likely weighed the same as an eight-pound human newborn. "One misconception people have about dinosaurs is that they laid these enormous eggs," Chiappe says. "They actually laid fairly small eggs for their size. The babies just grew incredibly fast."

TEENAGE T. REX

Speaking of fast, by the time *T. rex* reached its early teens, it had grown to more than 60 times its weight as a toddler. The husky teen imagined here weighed a whopping 4,000 pounds and measured 21 feet long.

Meet the Family

The renovated Dinosaur Hall at the Natural History Museum of Los Angeles County, in California, opened to the public in 2011. The hall's popular *T. rex* Growth Series features the fossils of a baby, teenager, and sub-adult *T. rex* nicknamed Thomas. The exhibit is currently the only one of its kind in the world, and the skeletons are among the youngest and most complete *T. rex* fossils ever discovered.

Fossils can tell us a lot about a creature's life. They can give us hints about the shape of an animal's body and its posture. Studying an animal's relatives can help fill in the gaps on the color and texture of its skin too. Artists at the museum's Dinosaur Institute work closely with scientists to create fleshed-out illustrations of the prehistoric beasts. They created the drawings of the tyrannosaur trio found on the previous page. But without soft tissue samples to draw from, it's hard to know for sure what *T. rex* looked like in life, says Chiappe. That's O.K.—for now, the fossils still have many untold tales to tell.

Dinosaur Hall
NATURAL HISTORY MUSEUM LOS ANGELES COUNTY, CALIFORNIA

SUB-ADULT T. REX

Nicknamed Thomas, this fossil was excavated in Carter County, Montana, between 2003 and 2005. At 17 years old, Thomas is believed to have weighed 7,000 pounds and measured 34 feet from head to tail. During its teen years, *T. rex* could gain up to an estimated 1,500 pounds a year. "This tells us that *T. rex*, like us, did not grow uniformly through time," Chiappe says.

While the series reveals a lot about how *T. rex* grew up, Chiappe says the exhibit intentionally leaves many questions open. "There are so many things about *T. rex* that we don't know," he says. "We hope kids going through the exhibit will be inspired to become paleontologists, so that they can one day dream of finding the evidence needed to answer those questions."

BABY T. REX

The fossil below was discovered in Garfield County, Montana, in the late 1960s and is likely the youngest *T. rex* fossil ever found. Scientists estimate that it was about 2 years old when it died. Visitors to the Dinosaur Hall will notice many differences in the proportions of the three skeletons. Adult *T. rexes* were not scaled up versions of their babies. For instance, if you look at the eye socket of the baby *T. rex*, you'll see that it is round. But when you look at Thomas's eye socket, it is shaped like a keyhole. The baby *T. rex* also has a longer skull and more slender limbs than its older exhibit companions. "The story of *T. rex* is one of transformation," says Chiappe.

TEENAGE T. REX

Unearthed around the same time and place as the baby *T. rex* fossil were the remains of an adolescent *T. rex*. This rare specimen was about 13 years old when it died and provides a key link to understanding the dino's rapid growth.

A Frozen World
Down Under

Antarctica is the coldest, windiest, and emptiest place on Earth. Its coast and waters are home to all kinds of fascinating marine life, from penguins and seals to whales and colossal squids. Deep-freeze conditions over millions of years have created an enormous ice sheet that covers the continent—the ice is nearly three miles thick in places! Yet, with less than two inches of rain or snow a year, Antarctica is also the world's largest desert. Temperatures can be bone-chillingly cold and vary by location, with the coast being warmer than the interior. The lowest reported temperature in Antarctica so far was a frosty −135.8°F.

But the subzero weather hasn't stopped tourists from visiting or scientists from conducting studies on the frozen continent. The National Science Foundation (NSF) funds polar research in both the Arctic and the Antarctic. The U.S. agency also makes it possible for journalists and photographers to visit. It invited TFK to go on an icy adventure to the bottom of the world. Read all about it here!

Gearing Up!

Those heading to the NSF's U.S. Antarctic Program's (USAP) McMurdo Station fly to Antarctica from Christchurch, New Zealand. The group TFK was part of flew on an aircraft called the LC-130 Hercules. It's a special plane outfitted with skis. The crews that fly these planes are from the New York State Air National Guard. The Guard has 10 planes and 26 crews that take USAP staff, scientists, and visitors on the eight-hour flight to and from the frozen continent.

All travelers must first stop by the USAP's warehouse of extreme cold weather gear. After all, the most important issue facing a visitor at the coldest place on the planet is what to wear! At the Clothing Distribution Center, in Christchurch, visitors pick up some polar essentials. The checklist includes gloves, hats, fleece jackets, extra-thick socks, wind pants, long underwear, and snow goggles. The warehouse is filled with row after row of specially insulated footwear, called bunny boots, and the iconic down-feather parka everyone wears, known as Big Red. Weather in the region can change suddenly, so it's best to be ready for anything!

BIRDS OF A FEATHER
Adélie penguins live on the mainland of Antarctica and on nearby islands. In the winter, the birds populate the sea ice, where food is plentiful. During the spring breeding season, they live in large colonies along the rocky coastline. Adélies line their nests with stones and have been known to steal rocks from their neighbors!

Cool Jobs

McMurdo Station is the largest of the U.S. research stations in Antarctica. A sign posted outside the dining hall at McMurdo tracks the exact number of people living there. During the summer months (November to February), McMurdo has a population of around 800 people. In winter, the population is less than 200. McMurdo is a small town, and many of its residents are scientists. "Each year, we send about 125 teams of scientists to our research stations in Antarctica," says the NSF's Peter West. But McMurdo is also home to carpenters, cooks, plumbers, pilots, and other people who help the station run smoothly.

The people who live and work in Antarctica learn not to take anything for granted. The only plants that grow there are mosses and tiny algae. Food, water, and fuel all have to be shipped or flown in. Then, every bit of garbage must be taken out the same way.

No country owns Antarctica. It is governed by the Antarctic Treaty System, which calls for the continent to be set aside for peaceful purposes and scientific exploration. Scientists there study everything from penguins and insects to meteorites and lava lakes. Here's a closer look at some of their work.

ON THE OPEN ICE

An emperor penguin mother lays a single egg in a season. The parents take turns watching over the egg and going to fish. The chicks are born with a warm coat of fuzzy feathers, called down. They shed the extra coat when they grow older. Each chick has a special call. This is how parents can tell which of the many chicks is theirs.

MAPPING ANTARCTICA

Cartographers, or mapmakers, use high-tech satellites to chart Antarctica's interior. But sometimes, the job still requires someone to put on boots and head out into the wild. Cole Kelleher (below) is familiar with this. He's a cartographer with the Polar Geospatial Center (PGC), which is based at the University of Minnesota.

PGC teamed up with Google to use the company's Trekker technology to capture images of Antarctica for the Internet giant's Street View map feature. To accomplish the task, Kelleher wore a Trekker camera on top of his backpack as he hiked the terrain. The camera records images in all directions. "It weighs about 50 pounds. I was out for two and a half days, hiking 10 to 12 hours each day," says Kelleher. "It was hard work but really an incredible experience."

SOUTH POLE SCIENCE

More than 100 years ago, the Norwegian explorer Roald Amundsen made history as the first person to reach the South Pole. Traveling to the Pole today has become more routine, but it is every bit as remarkable. A lot of important research is happening at the South Pole. Scientists study everything from changes in the atmosphere to deep space. For example, the South Pole Telescope is used to look at the universe far beyond what can be seen with the naked eye.

THE PENGUIN RODEO

Scientist Jean Pennycook (second from left) studies penguins. Each summer, she camps out in a tent on Cape Royds to observe Adélie colonies. Researchers get to the site by helicopter. Pennycook and her team put bands on the birds to help keep track of them. They do so by rounding up the penguins and gently placing the bands on the fuzzy chicks. "We call it the penguin rodeo," she says.

A MUMMY MYSTERY

Hundreds of mummified seals can be found scattered around Antarctica's Dry Valleys, a desert habitat of sand and rocks. But how did the marine animals end up so many miles from the sea? It's clear the animals got lost but not clear why. Once a seal ends up in the valleys, its body can be preserved by the dry cold for 1,000 years. Researchers study the mummies to find clues about the conditions in which the seals lived all those centuries ago.

THE STREAM TEAM

The Dry Valleys may be peppered with seal mummies, but they are far from lifeless! In this dry habitat are entire ecosystems of microscopic organisms that spring to life when water is added. For a few weeks each summer, the temperatures are warm enough to melt glacial ice, which can create streams. Colorful mats of bacteria grow along the streambeds and tiny organisms live in the surrounding damp soils. The organisms that live in the streams survive being freeze-dried most of the year.

Student Aneliya Sakaeva (right) is a member of a group called the "stream team." As part of their studies, the researchers collect water samples from the temporary streams as well as samples of the organisms that live there.

More than 3,300 years ago, a boy named Tutankhamun ruled Egypt. He ascended the throne around the age of 9 and ruled until his death 10 years later. Following his burial, the young pharaoh's reign appeared to have been erased from history. That is, until 1922, when British archaeologist Howard Carter unearthed Tut's tomb in the Valley of the Kings—and with it, Tut's mummified remains. Tutankhamun was not Egypt's most important or powerful ruler. But the story of the boy monarch, told through his mummy and his treasures, has fascinated generations. Here, All Access peels back the layers of the famed Egyptian king's tomb.

King Tut's Tomb

THINGS

Treasure and telephones and toys. Oh, my! Get an insider's glimpse at these cool collections and more.

Tut Unwrapped

1 FIRST SHRINE
The tomb had four main rooms, one of which was the burial chamber housing Tut's mummy. When members of Carter's team entered the burial chamber in 1923, they encountered a gleaming gold and blue shrine. It was the first of many surrounding Tut's body.

2 FRAME AND PALL
Underneath, the team found a wooden frame. The structure was covered in gold leaf, which is gold that has been hammered into a thin foil. A linen pall, or cloth, bedazzled with metallic sequins, hung over the top beams.

3 SECOND SHRINE
It's possible this monument was intended for a different royal. The hieroglyphs spelling out *Tutankhamun* had been etched over another name—likely his predecessor's.

4 THIRD SHRINE
This shrine featured a sloping roof and gold-leaf exterior, just like the one before it. All four shrines had funerary texts engraved on the walls. Ancient Egyptians believed the writings would assist the departed in the afterlife.

5 FOURTH SHRINE
Images of ancient Egyptian gods and goddesses, including the falcon-headed sky lord Horus, decorated this last shrine. Horus was the guardian of kings.

6 SARCOPHAGUS
By 1924, Carter had finally reached Tut's stone sarcophagus. Winged goddesses were displayed at the corners, standing guard over the pharaoh.

7 FIRST COFFIN
The sarcophagus held three nested coffins bearing the king's image. The outermost vessel was built from wood and finished with sheets of gold.

8 SECOND COFFIN
Gold leaf, gemstones, and colored glass adorned this striking middle casket.

9 THIRD COFFIN
The innermost coffin was truly fit for royalty. It was made of solid gold!

10 THE MUMMY
Ancient Egyptians preserved bodies through a process known as mummification. They used spices, salts, minerals, and oils to treat the body and then wrapped it in strips of cloth. Tut's mummy is the most famous of all. Found among the king's bandages were nearly 150 jewels and charms, including a magnificent gold mask. In 2007, scientists moved the fragile mummy to a glass case to protect it from heat and moisture. It was the first time in history that the public had seen Tut's unwrapped face.

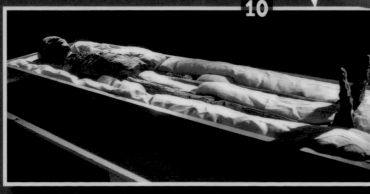

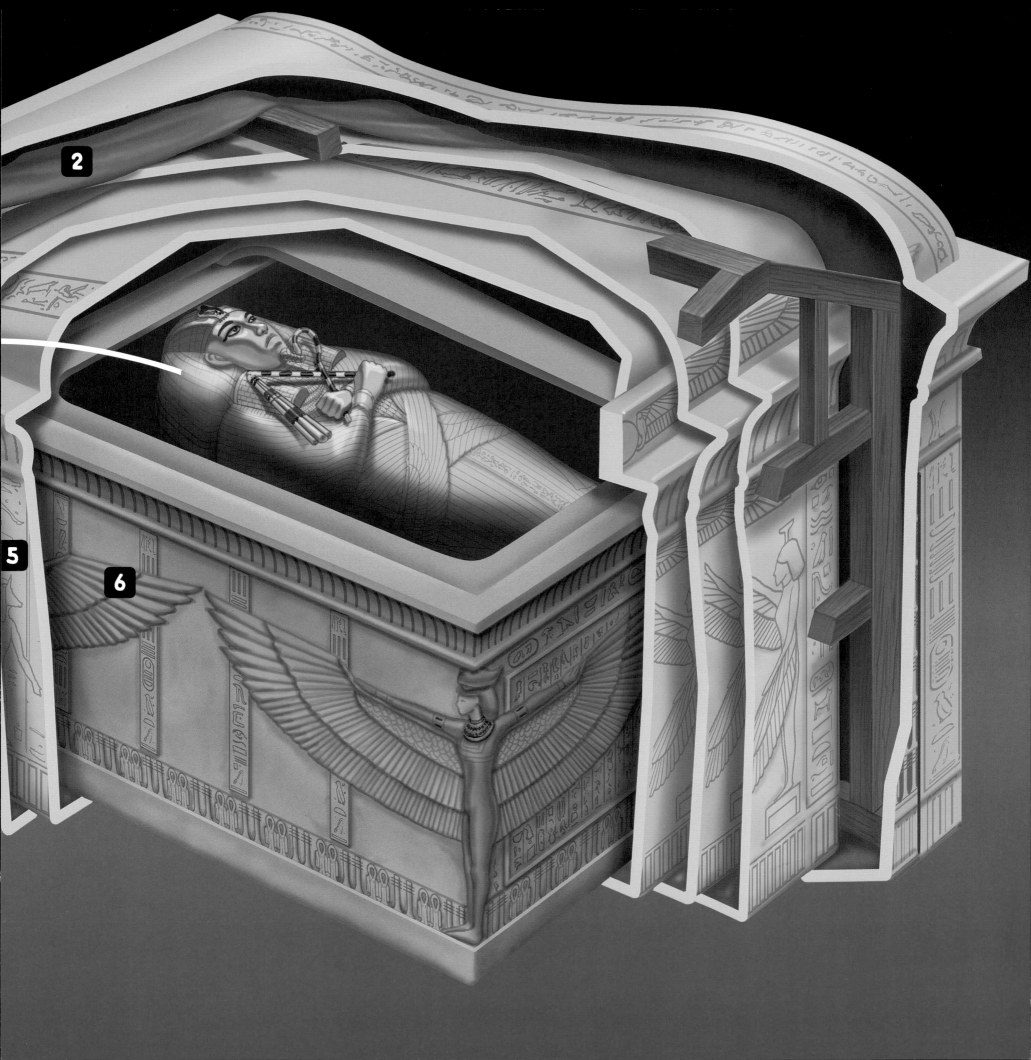

Golden Goodies

What does a boy king need in the afterlife? Quite a lot, judging by the more than 5,000 artifacts discovered in Tutankhamun's tomb. Ancient Egyptians filled the resting places of their departed rulers with mounds of gold, jewels, and other valuables. The treasure attracted many thieves—most royal tombs had been cleaned out by the time they were found. Not King Tut's, however. When archaeologist Howard Carter uncovered the young pharaoh's tomb thousands of years after it was sealed, he found it almost completely intact. Because of this, Tut's tomb proved to be one of the greatest discoveries of the 20th century. These are just a few of the relics found inside.

SWEET CHARIOT

Six chariots were found among the items, but only this one displayed signs of actual use. In fact, Tut may have fallen off this same chariot and broken his leg. Some experts believe complications from the broken limb and from malaria likely led to the teen's untimely death.

FANCY FOOTWEAR

A pair of golden sandals was found on the feet of Tut's mummy when it was unwrapped. The mummy was also wearing gold finger and toe coverings.

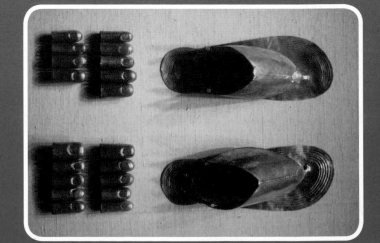

THE MASK

Covering the head of Tut's mummy was this royal death mask made of pure gold, glass, and gems. Today, it's the most recognized of King Tut's artifacts.

CROWNING MOMENT

Tut wore this golden diadem in life and in death. The crown, inlaid with glass and gemstones, features a cobra and a vulture—symbols of Tut's rule. The charms were removed from the headdress during the burial, however, possibly so the death mask would fit.

BEASTS BEWARE

One of the many objects found on the body of Tut's mummy was a ceremonial dagger and sheath. Zahi Hawass, a top Egyptian archaeologist, has explained in interviews that the dagger was provided to allow Tut to defend himself from wild beasts in the afterlife.

GIVE IT A REST!

This ivory headrest is one of several found in Tut's tomb. It's no ordinary pillow, though. Ancient Egyptians believed that headrests held magic that protected the head in the afterlife. This one features Shu, the god of air. The two lions symbolize the eastern and western horizons, where the sun rises and sets.

ALL HANDS ON DECK!

Royal figures were often buried with small statues of servants, called *ushabti* (oo-*shab*-tee). Ancient Egyptians believed these figures would help perform agricultural duties for the ruler in the afterlife. Tut's tomb contained more than 400 ushabti statues.

GAME ON

Sure, Tut reigned over Egypt, but he was still a kid too. Kids like to play, and this boy king was no different. From the number of game boards found in the tomb, it seems one of his favorite activities was a game called Senet. The word *senet* means "passing." The exact rules of the two-player game are unknown, but the aim was to pass your pieces off the board faster than your opponent.

The Telephone

Hello?

The phone has been transformed over the years. See if any of these models from the past and present ring a bell.

1876

LIQUID TRANSMITTER

"Mr. Watson, come here! I want you." Alexander Graham Bell speaks these famous first words into an experimental phone, like this one, on March 10, 1876. His creation forever changes the way we communicate.

1892

WESTERN ELECTRIC FOLDING CABINET DESK SET

These desk phones—also known as vanity sets—are found mostly in public spaces, such as hotel lobbies and offices. The phone's base is bolted to the top of the desk, and the circuits are tucked inside.

1919

ROTARY DIAL PHONE

The first rotary dial phones date back to the 1890s. But it isn't until 1919 that more American consumers start giving them a spin. Before this dialing system came along, a switchboard operator acted as a middleman to connect calls. Now customers call one another directly.

1970s

TOUCH-TONE PHONE

By the 1960s and '70s, a new phone design begins taking over the industry, ending the long reign of the rotary dial. Touch-tone technology makes for easier dialing and fewer finger fumbles.

MOTOROLA STARTAC

More than 10 years after the DynaTAC debuts, Motorola presents another first in the world of mobile phones: the first clamshell-style handset. Small, light, and sleek, the StarTAC becomes the must-have phone of its time.

T-MOBILE G1

These *are* the Droids you're looking for. The T-Mobile G1 is the first cell phone to use the Android operating system. More than a billion Android-powered phones are activated in the five years following the G1's introduction, making Android the most popular mobile operating system around.

MOTOROLA DYNATAC 8000X

The world's first commercial mobile phone isn't all that, well, mobile. Nicknamed the brick phone (for good reason), the Motorola DynaTAC 8000x weighs about two pounds and comes with a whopping $3,995 price tag for the handset alone.

1983

1996

2008

1993

2007

2013

IBM SIMON

It may not look the part, but IBM's Simon is the original smartphone. The touch-screen-operated device is an all-in-one phone, fax machine, pager, and computer. It even has apps. A memory card plugged into the phone gives users access to a camera, maps, games, music, and more.

APPLE iPHONE (FIRST GENERATION)

The iPhone isn't the first mobile device to feature a touch screen. But its innovative, keyboard-less design sets off a craze that ushers in a new age of touch-screen phones.

SAMSUNG GALAXY GEAR

The Galaxy Gear Smartwatch takes hands-free to a new level. This stylish companion to the Galaxy line of smartphones allows wearers to receive calls, text messages, and e-mails, all from the wrist.

Toy Story

No, it's not the Disney store. But it could easily be mistaken for it! Step inside the office of Pixar's head honcho, John Lasseter, where toys rule.

WORK HARD, PLAY HARD

An avid collector, Lasseter (right) is as passionate about toys as he is about making movies. Thousands of figurines cover every inch of his office—from some of his cherished childhood dolls to scores of Pixar action figures. And there's even more in storage!

TO INFINITY, AND BEYOND!

The collection wouldn't be complete without Woody and Buzz, the stars of Disney/Pixar's 1995 animated feature *Toy Story*. The characters were inspired by two of Lasseter's favorite toys from when he was a boy. Woody was based on a pull-string doll of Casper the Friendly Ghost; Buzz, on a G.I. Joe. He still has both, of course.

THE CAT'S MEOW

Recognize this furry grin? It's the Cat Bus, from the classic Japanese animated film *My Neighbor Totoro*. The stuffed cartoon kitty was a gift from director pal Hayao Miyazaki.

ALL ABOARD!

Lasseter shows off some of the prized locomotives that line his shelves. More of his collection is in his home in Sonoma, California, where model trains run on tracks throughout the house. He even built a train library, accessed only by a secret door that leads to a hidden staircase.

Meet Lady Liberty

S he's the most recognizable lady in the United States, and possibly even in the world. That's right. We're talking about Lady Liberty. The Statue of Liberty was a gift of friendship from France to the United States in 1886. French sculptor Frédéric-Auguste Bartholdi designed the iconic monument. He called it "Liberty Enlightening the World."

The Statue of Liberty stands tall on Liberty Island in New York Harbor, near the onetime immigration port of Ellis Island. From 1892 to 1954, more than 12 million immigrants entered America through New York City. Lady Liberty—a towering beacon of freedom and democracy—was the first to welcome them to the country.

Bartholdi and his assistants spent nine years building the statue. The final structure stands about 305 feet tall from the ground to the tip of the torch. It weighs 225 tons, or 450,000 pounds—that's as heavy as 30 elephants! France held various fund-raising events to raise money for the statue's $250,000 price tag.

In 1878, the monument's completed head was shown at the Paris World's Fair. Once Bartholdi finished the statue, the tricky part was getting it from France to its final destination in New York. Workers disassembled it into 350 parts and packed them in 214 crates. On the voyage across the Atlantic, a powerful storm nearly sank the ship carrying the pieces. But the statue arrived safely at its new home in June 1885. After the pedestal was completed, it was reassembled in four months' time.

Today, Lady Liberty greets thousands of visitors from around the globe daily. Check out this inside—and outside—look at the Statue of Liberty.

STAIRCASE
There are a total of 354 steps from the ground floor up to the crown. One hundred sixty-two of those steps are inside the statue. A narrow spiral staircase in the home stretch leads visitors to the crown.

Cashing In

Dollar bills. They're used every day to pay for things—school lunches, clothes, toys, you name it. But have you ever thought about where money actually comes from and how it's made? (Hint: It doesn't grow on trees!) The U.S. Bureau of Engraving and Printing (BEP) has been making the nation's paper currency since 1862. Each year, BEP facilities in Washington, D.C., and in Fort Worth, Texas, churn out billions of notes worth billions of dollars. It takes hundreds of highly skilled workers and a mix of modern technology and traditional printing techniques to create the valuable bills. Here's a peek at the process.

The Green Machine

1 BLENDING IN

Crane & Co. is the sole supplier of currency paper for the BEP. The sheets are made of 75% cotton and 25% linen. This special blend gives U.S. bills a unique look and feel. The cotton is boiled in a large kettle before being processed into paper at the company's mill, in Dalton, Massachusetts. A single sheet can make 32 bills.

2 START THE PRESSES!

The first step in the money-making process is called offset printing. At this stage, the bills are given their background colors. Each sheet of paper is fed through a large machine that prints strips of colors on the front and back of the bills. The sheets dry for 72 hours before going on to the next step, intaglio (in-*tal*-ee-oh) printing. *Intaglio* means "to engrave" in Italian. Intaglio plates (below) are used to print portraits, lettering, and numbers on the notes.

3 THE COLOR OF MONEY

All bills use green ink. But if you look closely, you'll notice that notes valued $5 and up also feature other colors that are unique to each denomination: purple and gray are on the $5 bill; orange, yellow, and red on the $10; peach and blue on the $20; blue and red on the $50; and gold and copper on the $100. (Turn the page for a closer look at the new $100 note.) Color-shifting ink is also used on currency valued $10 and higher. In 2013, the BEP used approximately 9.6 tons of ink per day.

4 QUALITY CONTROL

Throughout the printing process, BEP workers carefully examine the sheets to make sure the color is perfect and the markings are accurate. If there are imperfections, a sheet is discarded, and the workers must find and fix the problem before printing can continue.

5 DOWN FOR THE COUNT

The BEP tracks every single sheet of currency paper from start to finish. Workers are constantly inspecting the stacks to make sure all the sheets are accounted for.

6 CASHING OUT

During the final part of the printing process, the bills are stamped with the Federal Reserve and Treasury seals, serial numbers, and the Federal Reserve identification numbers. Then they are cut and bundled for delivery. In 2013, the BEP delivered approximately 6.6 billion bills to 12 Federal Reserve banks across the country. From there, the money gets sent to local banks.

Big Ben

Benjamin Franklin is sporting a smart—and colorful—look these days. On October 8, 2013, the U.S. Federal Reserve released a redesigned $100 bill chock-full of high-tech security updates. These measures will make it easier to spot a real $100 note. They will also make it harder to counterfeit, or create fake money. More than a decade of research went into the revamp. This is the bill's first major makeover since 1996. So, what are some of these fancy new features? Let's dig in.

THE MAN HIMSELF

The portrait of Benjamin Franklin remains the same as the one used on the current $100 bill, but the image is slightly bigger on the new note. The dark oval surrounding the engraving is also gone. Microtext has been added to Franklin's collar and along the bill's top right corner.

NEW THREADS

A new security thread embedded on the left side of the bill can be seen when held up to the light. The number *100* and the word *USA* are printed on the thread in an alternating pattern. The thread turns pink under ultraviolet light.

NEW VIEW

A portrait of Independence Hall remains on the back. But instead of an image of the front of the hall, as it appears on the current bill, the new bill shows an image of the back of the building.

Through the Years

The $100 bill has received many face-lifts over the past century. Check out how much it has changed.

1890

1914

BLUE-RIBBON DAY

The change people might notice immediately is the blue ribbon running vertically to the right of Franklin's portrait. This 3-D strip is found on only the front of the bill and is woven in through a top-secret process. When tilted, the bells found on the ribbon change to 100s.

FREEDOM QUILL

In addition to the inkwell, a golden feather quill has been added to the front of the bill. The quill represents the one used by the Founding Fathers to sign the Declaration of Independence.

THE WATERMARK

Hold the bill up to the light, and you'll find a smaller, simplified portrait of Franklin staring right back at you. He might look a bit blurry, though. The special paper on which U.S. currency is printed makes watermarks appear fuzzy.

CHANGE OF COLOR

The new bill features color-shifting ink that changes from copper to green when the note is tilted. This special ink contains microscopic flakes that reflect different colors in the light. It can be found on the 100 on the lower right corner on the front, as well as on the new inkwell image.

1922

1928

1996

Image Credits

COVER: International Space Station: NASA; background photo: Getty Images; Astronaut: Smiley Pool for TIME For Kids; capsule: Boeing/NASA

INSIDE COVER: Background: Getty Images; astronaut: Smiley Pool for TIME For Kids

CONTENTS: Background photo: Getty Images; photos from top to bottom: Smithsonian's National Zoo; Metropolitan Transportation Authority; Deborah Coleman/Pixar

PAGES 4-7: Background: Getty Images; Astronaut: Smiley Pool for TIME For Kids

PAGES 8-9: International Space Center: Science Photo Library/Getty Images; photos: NASA

PAGES 10-13: All photos: Deborah Boardley/96 Greene Mgmt.

PAGES 14-15: AF archive /Alamy; headshot: Frazer Harrison/Getty Images for the British Film Commission

PAGES 16-17: Left to right: Mark Tantrum/WireImage; Steve Granitz/WireImage; Hagen Hopkins/Getty Images; Warren Little/Getty Images; Dave J. Hogan/Getty Images; Luca Teuchmann/Getty Images; Barry King/FilmMagic; Dave M. Benett/Getty Images (3); Hagen Hopkins/Getty Images; Mike Marsland/WireImage; Steve Granitz/WireImage

PAGES 18-21: Photos: Smithsonian's National Zoo; illustrations from the Washington Post, August 26 © 2013 Washington Post Company

PAGES 22-25: White House: Dan Taylor/Destination 360; Miniature White House photos: Todd Bigelow for TIME For Kids

PAGES 26-27: Google Campus: Erin Lubin/Bloomberg via Getty Images; library, NYC apartment office, car conference room: Eric Laignel; Google server room: Connie Zhou/Google; bicycle, sliding board: courtesy Google; golf course: Reuters/Mark Blinch; nap pod: Reuters/Erin Siegal; tunnel conference room: Reuters/Arnd Wiegmann

PAGES 28-29: Illustration by John Walker

PAGES 30-31: Illustration by John Walker; Amazon spread: top to bottom, left to right: Juniors Bildarchiv GmbH/Alamy; SamboPhoto/Getty Images; ThePalmer/Getty Images; Tui De Roy/Getty Images; Amazon-Images /Alamy; Javier Garcia; Thomas Marent/Visuals Unlimited, Inc./Getty Images; Roy Toft/Getty Images; Margie Politzer/Getty Images; Martin Shields/Getty Images; Andoni Canela/Getty Images; Danita Delimont/Getty Images; Ben Queenborough/Getty Images; Mint Images/Frans Lanting/Getty Images; Mark Bowler/Getty Images; Getty Images

PAGES 32-35: All photos © Metropolitan Transportation Authority

PAGES 36-37: Dinosaur illustrations by Stephanie Abramowicz/Natural History Museum of Los Angeles County; background illustration by John Walker

PAGES 38-39: Kayte Deioma/Zumapress

PAGES 40-41: Main image: Kevin Schafer/Minden Pictures; inset: David Bjerklie for TIME For Kids

PAGES 42-43: Background: Norbert Wu/Minden Pictures/Getty Images; maps by Joe Lemonnier for TIME For Kids; clockwise from top left: Cole Kelleher/Polar Geospatial Center; Elaine Hood/NSF; Peter West/NSF; Peter Rejcek; Emily Stone/NSF

PAGES 44-45: Illustration by John Walker; mask: The Image Bank/Getty Images

PAGES 46-47: Illustration by John Walker; mummy: Reportage/Archival Image/Alamy

PAGES 48-49: Footwear: Universal History Archive; chariot: Lebrecht Music and Arts Photo Library/Alamy; mask: The Image Bank/Getty Images; headrest: CULNAT, Dist. RMN-GP/Art Resource,NY; Ushabti figure: DeAgostini/Getty Images; diadem: AP Photo/Ric Francis; daggers: The Bridgeman Art Library/Getty Images; game: Art Media/Print Collector/Getty Images

PAGES 50-51: Left to right, top to bottom: Getty Images; Ryan McVay/Getty Images; Tim Boyle/Bloomberg via Getty Images; Science & Society Picture Library/Getty Images; AP Photo/Mark Lennihan; John Jenkins; Steve Wisbauer/Getty Images; IBM; Gabriel Bouys/AFP/Getty Images; Samsung

PAGES 52-53: All photos: Deborah Coleman/Pixar

PAGES 54-55: Alex Segre/Alamy; inset: Stan Honda/AFP/Getty Images

PAGES 56-57: Illustrations by Patrick Gnan

PAGES 58-59: From left clockwise: AP Photo/LM Otero; Crane & Company; Marvin Joseph/The Washington Post via Getty Images; Kristoffer Tripplaar/Alamy; AP Photo/LM Otero; Alex Wong/Getty Images; AP Photo/LM Otero

PAGES 60-61: 1928 hundred dollar bill: National Numismatic Collection at the Smithsonian Institution

BACK INSIDE COVER: Getty Images

BACK COVER: Book: background: Getty Images, astronaut: Smiley Pool for TIME For Kids; funerary mask: The Image Bank/Getty; penguins: Norbert Wu/Minden Pictures/Getty Images